TEACHER
TO
TEACHER
Publications

Talk
Talk
Talk:
DISCUSSION-BASED
CLASSROOMS

ANN COOK and PHYLLIS TASHLIK

ANN COOK: SERIES EDITOR

TEACHERS
COLLEGE
PRESS

COMMUNITY STUDIES, INC

Grateful acknowledgement to the Bill and Melinda Gates Foundation and
Community Studies, Inc. for support provided

Distributed by Teachers College Press, 1234 Amsterdam Avenue, New York, NY 10027

ISBN 0-8077-4563-4

Manufactured in the United States of America

11 10 09 08 07 06 05 04   8 7 6 5 4 3 2 1

CONTENTS

Introduction

When teachers meet, they usually feel comfortable exchanging ideas about literacy and ways to help students read and write well. These are the skills they were taught as students, the ones most emphasized in professional training courses, by the media, and in statewide assessments.

By contrast, discussion and the techniques that best support effective dialogue are seldom the focus of professional conversation. It's interesting to speculate why, since we do know that kids like to talk. Is it because few teachers themselves experienced genuine discussion when they were students and, therefore, have no personal experiences to draw on? Or is it because discussion skills are almost totally neglected by teacher education programs, leaving teachers to gain skills on the job?

Both are possibilities. Another may be that oral communication skills are downgraded because they don't factor into state assessments. Most states mimic New York, which acknowledges "speaking" as one of its four key language arts learning standards, but then relegates it to oblivion by making absolutely no attempt to assess it.

And because discussion is devalued, most teachers readily admit reluctance to assign it a central role. If they are honest, many go even further, expressing skepticism about its purpose. They doubt that student talk serves any function other than as an introductory activity signaling a new topic for study, or as an icebreaker designed to grab students' attention before the "real" lesson begins.

The idea that discussion should feature prominently in the learning process—indeed occupy center stage as a teaching strategy—is quite foreign to most educators.

"Why would you want to do that?" is a common response, followed by, "Besides, students don't know enough."

Others ask: "If student talk is central, what's the teacher's role?" And: "Shouldn't a teacher just tell students what they need to know instead of wasting valuable time?"

Answers to questions like these depend on what one's beliefs are about how students learn, how they take in and understand information, and what a teacher's role is in helping further that understanding. When professionals set a premium on discussion as the best tool for helping kids use their minds well, they are also, both directly and indirectly, defining their value system, helping to create the culture of the school, and advocating particular teaching strategies. Teachers who set a premium on achieving high scores on state exit exams will, in contrast, evolve a very different value system, school culture, and set of teaching strategies.

To develop a culture that supports discussion, professionals too will need time to discuss. By engaging in meaningful dialogue with each other, they learn to value meaningful dialogue for their students. After observing classrooms where authentic discussion among students occurs, they will want to replicate that experience in their own classrooms. We believe that the more professionals are exposed to the excitement and stimulation of discussion-based classrooms, the more committed they will be to supporting its values and strategies in their own classrooms.

By featuring student discussion and interviews as well as teacher interviews, the film, *Talk, Talk, Talk: Discussion-Based Classrooms* demonstrates how a professional culture influences the day-to-day exchanges between student and teacher, teacher and teacher. The practices demonstrated and discussed in the film are also strengthened through practices not observable, such as staff and curriculum meetings and the training program teachers have developed for new teachers joining their staff (more on this later in Chapter 7).

The teachers featured in this film have found that the most meaningful professional development occurs when they share practices, student work, and problems at their staff and curriculum meetings; when they visit each other's classrooms or team teach; when they attend student presentations and defenses; and when they continually review assessment criteria and challenge each other's ideas. From this they have evolved the common language, goals, and beliefs you see and hear in the film. The staff is immersed in a type of professional discussion that supports and reinforces the value of discussion for both themselves and their students.

1

What Do We Mean by Discussion?

"With this type of learning I'm active—I'm actually saying stuff, I'm doing stuff—other students are active and they're doing stuff."

Dakota, student

Even if there is consensus about making time for discussion, there isn't always agreement about what we mean by "discussion." A lesson that moves through a given body of material and uses discussion to reach a preordained set of conclusions will, at best, generate a dull conversation; at worst, it will promote a cynical response and reinforce rote learning.

Contrast that with a discussion centered on an open-ended question, one that has no specifically right or wrong answer but rather invites thoughtful responses and controversy. Now that could cause problems of "control." A lively debate among students based on real disagreements might lead to friction both in and out of class. Or may require more knowledge about a topic than a teacher has readily available. Teachers worry about such issues, and it's easy to see why.

But students, particularly those accustomed to discussion-based classrooms, readily identify student-to-student talk as one key factor in making learning meaningful. They point to the importance of being able to express their point of view, work through ideas, listen to others, change their mind, and formulate new questions as key factors that engage their interest and foster understanding. Students make a strong case for classrooms where active participation is a centerpiece.

As one of the students familiar with discussion-based classrooms explained, "In traditional classes, the teacher is always presenting her ideas; when you're in that environment your mind doesn't work—you just receive the information and that's it. When you're in discussion-based classes, you still receive information but you're also processing it and questioning it."

Other students have told us, "In discussion classes you really learn—you get really deep into a subject. I think it's interesting, and I think you actually learn instead of memorizing. You learn a lot more."

And, ". . . it stays with you. A lot of stuff you get taught at other schools you remember for that week. The next week you ask yourself: What did they say again?"

Why This Film?

The dilemma is how to convince teachers to take up the challenge—to organize classes around inquiry-based discussions and promote greater student engagement.

We believe that images can play a powerful role in encouraging teachers to embark on that challenge. *Talk, Talk, Talk* is a response to teachers' queries about what inquiry-based discussions look like and what teachers and students who have participated in them say about the experience.

The film makes clear why discussion matters and why it is a particularly effective way to engage and sustain student interest while, at the same time, providing a framework that supports deeper understanding.

We suggest viewing the film first, then using this booklet as a supplement; it offers more details and examples from actual discussion-based classrooms. Our hope is that the film will raise questions about discussion—about the role of the teacher, about inquiry, about the conditions that foster authentic discussion—and that this booklet will help answer questions that might arise for teachers interested in exploring these issues further.

What is the Difference Between Information-Based and Discussion-Based Teaching?

"At this school, you're constantly asked, Why? and Can you prove it?"

Marcela, student

THE TRADITIONAL APPROACH The traditional approach to teaching centers on information acquisition. As the principal of a small NYC public high school explains: "In the traditional approach, a teacher prepares a lesson in a content area, which would have a beginning and a middle and an end. Prepared questions permit the teacher to lead students through the requisite materials. The teacher has a specific goal in mind and, if successful, would reach that goal by covering the materials by the end of the period (usually 45 minutes). The kids should be able to summarize the material and acquire the prescribed body of information that was presented to them.

"The inquiry process is nothing like that."

When the drive to "cover" material is paramount, little time is left to discover. Discussion is cursory or, worse, a contest to see which student can come up with the "right" answer—the one already in the teacher's head. The discussion direction is pre-determined with few surprises.

In inquiry, what you're trying to do is take a question that has no pre-scribed answer and frame that question so that there's genuine specu-lation, debate, and discussion. The teacher often presents conflicting evidence and asks students to examine materials, draw conclusions, and support those conclusions in thoughtful discussions with others who (using the same evidence) may have reached divergent conclusions.

Real discussion has everything to do with the question posed. It occurs when responses to the question are unpredictable, when the questions asked lead to new questions that weren't there when the class first began, when more than one response seems reasonable—or can be reasonably argued—and when students are drawn into the conversa-tion, compelled to participate by speaking up or listening attentively.

Teachers comfortable with discussion-based classrooms explain their role as "leading a discussion by asking more questions that lead students to critique what they have already said." Further, they point out that the value of talk is frequently *talk*. As one teacher explained, "It's the saying of something aloud that actually helps to clarify think-ing and learning. Ideas can be unformed or dormant in your mind until you have the opportunity to say them. Writing and talking are similar in this way—they provide a means of expression and clarifying knowl-edge."

The chart below points out the differences between the informa-tion-based and discussion-based approaches to the classroom and the effect of each on inquiry.

Information-Based Approach	Discussion-Based Approach
Each lesson has (in the teacher's mind) a clear beginning, middle, and end.	The teacher has long-range goals in mind. Although each lesson will not have neat closure, over time the larger themes and issues—as well as their complexities—emerge.
A distinct body of knowledge, as determined by the impossibly voluminous content covered in state exams, is "covered," usually through lectures, notes on the board, and textbook readings.	Course content may be planned by the teacher in the beginning, but its direction can be changed by evidence of student interest and engagement. Questions raised by students during class discussion can influence content of the course.
Students focus on figuring out what the teacher wants them to remember for the next test or what the state exam will require them to memorize.	The teacher nurtures an inquiry-based classroom. Students become active participants rather than passive recipients. Depth, rather than breadth, becomes the goal; students become proficient in particular areas of knowledge, sacrificing broad but superficial approaches to content in favor of in-depth exploration and understanding.
Students and teachers rely primarily on one textbook.	Students are exposed to multiple readings, not simply a single textbook rendering. Multiple points of view are presented, contrasted, discussed—this is true for all subject areas.

Information-Based Approach	Discussion-Based Approach
The teacher leads the students through a series of questions that have a predetermined "correct" answer (textbooks often supply these answers in teachers' editions, though the majority of teachers do not limit themselves to textbook renderings of correctness).	The teacher uses early questions to open up discussion and discover the best angle for engaging the particular group of students in that class. The questions do not have "correct" answers, only thoughtful ones.
Most of the exchanges occur between individual students and the teacher.	Students are encouraged to respond to what each other has said; the teacher's position is to restate, clarify, provide needed information, or tie together what has been said.
	The teacher's task is to continue to find the questions that will provoke thoughtful discussion, not to present questions where the answer is already determined. This presumes that the teacher has real questions, some of which may elude even the teacher.
	The teacher shows how students' contributions relate to each other, to the materials read and studied, and to the question the teacher had presented initially.

Information-Based Approach	Discussion-Based Approach
Students focus on figuring out what the teacher wants them to remember for the next test or what the state exam will require them to memorize.	In the classroom, because of the involvement of students in the discussion, all students are focused on processing the information presented, analyzing and critiquing what's been said, formulating new questions and ideas. This is true even for the student who has chosen to be quiet and not speak up in class.
Students' personal investment in the subject matter is generally nil.	Students participate and ask questions not to figure out what the teacher has in mind, but to understand the subject being discussed and their own, and each other's, ideas about it. They delve into subject matter to explore and *find out*.
Students let their teacher know what they have learned through incremental tests or a final exam. Not understanding something therefore translates into a punishment, since the student's test grade will suffer.	By using continual discussion in the classroom, the teacher hears what the students are thinking and how they are processing the information and content. The teacher does not have to rely on an exam to find out and respond to what students may have misunderstood or had difficulty with.

Information-Based Approach	Discussion-Based Approach
	When students can discuss an issue in depth, they help to clarify for themselves and others what they know. The complexities of a subject become more apparent and students develop a deeper investment in their learning.
Students are rarely expected to develop, let alone defend, their own perspective of the material covered.	Students become more analytic and critical. When multiple points of view are expressed in the classroom setting, students begin to weigh one argument against another and learn how to evaluate and develop criteria for criticism. They develop confidence in their ability to defend their opinions, even if they are in the minority.

4   How Are Classes Organized Around Discussion?

"If you don't teach using inquiry, it's hard to understand the role of the teacher. I'm not controlling what the kids say, I'm scaffolding the discussion, making on-going decisions about how to structure the discussion and organize the way ideas are talked about."

Avram Barlowe, teacher

Discussion-based classes require time and discipline. Though more open-ended than information-based pedagogy allows for, they are not free-for-alls.

Students, for example, once immersed in a discussion, might often repeat what has previously been said. This occurs because the saying of it is what helps the students to learn. Also, when students feel comfortable asking questions about what's on their mind concerning a topic, the discussion can take an unexpected direction. The teacher must make a judgment call: either to bring the discussion back to the original focus, make clear the connection between the new and previous direction, or wait it out and, as often happens, hear from a student who refocuses the discussion or presents the missing link among the disparate ideas on the floor.

During discussions, the teacher's role is complex: continually linking ideas, pointing out similarities and contrasts, posing new questions that have arisen as a result of the discussion or reframing what has been said.

The teacher must allow for the gradual unfolding of ideas, complexities, contradictions, and points of view. This takes time. The teacher does not impose his or her opinion, but does provide evidence from a variety of sources of others' writings or opinions or problem-solving techniques. The juxtaposition of readings from different points of view, in itself, stirs controversy for students. In addition, inquiry teachers will often invite knowledgeable adults with contrasting opinions to meet with students, answer their questions and pose new ones for consideration. Guest speakers are usually astounded by the subtlety of questions raised by students who are accustomed to discussing issues of importance in depth. For example, after a science class visit to a major wildlife center in NYC, the director—whom the students had interviewed—commended their participation, noting, "The students were extremely well prepared and I have to say that I have never been asked more insightful questions by anyone. It is always a pleasure to meet students who have gone beyond just 'handling' school to becoming educated in the most meaningful sense of the word."

In inquiry, teachers must learn to embrace neutrality. Although inquiry-based classes often focus on controversial ideas and questions, teachers are not there to promote a particular point of view. Whether or not teachers embrace the position of authority figure in the classroom, their opinion can greatly influence students. Since the goal is to help students make up their own minds, it's critically important to sidestep situations that might interfere with that process. The teacher's role in a discussion-based classroom (indeed, in any good classroom) is to present students with a wide range of divergent opinions, reliable texts and materials, and the time to discuss, probe, question, and think about the ramifications of all these materials so that they can make up their own minds and opinions.

What Techniques and Tools Develop and Support Discussion?

"There's a real respect among students and I think it's because we're taught that that's the way it is from the moment we step into this school."

Leta, student

MANTRAS:

"NO PERSONAL ATTACKS" AND "WHAT IS YOUR EVIDENCE?"

Two "mantras" guide the discussion-based classroom.

The first: No Personal Attacks. You may attack a person's ideas, but you may not attack the person. Students must respect a person's right to hold and express an opinion contrary to their own. They have no difficulty learning the difference between a personal attack and an attack of ideas. Students call "foul" whenever the former occurs, and teachers need to be quick to acknowledge and repudiate any verbal bullying disguised as informed opinion. Students experienced in discussion-based classes are quite effective guardians of such protocols especially when such comments are direct and verbal. More skill is required when attacks are subtle or non-verbal, such as derisive laughter or negative body language. In those cases teachers need to respond to protect divergent opinions and ensure an atmosphere of trust.

The second mantra, equal in importance to the first, is, What Is Your Evidence?

Inquiry arguments require examples, specifics, and details to support them. Students learn that during class discussions and will challenge each other, and their teachers, for the evidence to support a point of view. Assigned readings, homework assignments, and research they have conducted should provide a body of evidence on which to draw.

Discussion in which students are required to support their opinions with evidence keeps the conversation focused and helps students gain the skills necessary to handle divergent points of view. As one student explained, "You're sitting in a classroom thinking, I don't agree with that. But then you ask yourself, Why don't I agree? And I know I have to provide evidence to defend my point of view. I think that supporting your ideas with evidence is what promotes learning in the classes."

OPENING QUESTIONS AND THE "SORT"

Opening up, rather than narrowing down, discussion requires a good first question or activity. In science, that might mean asking students to carefully observe a phenomena without first explaining how it came to be, then asking them for their hypotheses. In literature, that might mean asking students if they're enjoying or not enjoying an assigned novel; the "not enjoying" response—when honestly presented—often opens up the most interesting and analytical of discussions. Or the question might focus on the broad impression of a character ("Is this narrator mad?") or a theme ("Do you believe that fate determines our lives?") or a value judgment ("What is good writing?")

Aside from the opening question, productive discussion can be launched by an activity—one designed to provoke an appreciation for the complexity of an issue. This might be accomplished by an activity known as a "sort."

A sort requires students to work individually and then in small groups. Initially students are asked to respond to a broad question, such as *Who are the ten most and ten least important figures in American history?* In this sort, each student would be given an envelope containing 70-80 small pieces of paper; written on each is the name of an important figure in history, or simply a well-known figure. For example, among the names that might be included in addition to Abraham Lincoln and George Washington are:

Henry Ford	Louis Armstrong
Eugene Debs	Margaret Sanger
"Deep Throat"	Elvis Presley
Huey Long	Sojourner Truth
Jacqueline Onassis	Muhammad Ali

Students are first asked to consider the choices on an individual basis, then to select the ten most and least important people in the country's history. (They can also add names if they choose.)

Following their individual selections, students form small groups (three or four students per group works best) to discuss their choices and produce a group selection of the five most and least important individuals. To reach such a group decision, of course, requires a good deal of sharing and discussion about the criteria used by each member of the group.

Eventually, each group presents its selections and rationales and the class as a whole then attempts to reach consensus about whom it would choose as the top and bottom three individuals.

Clearly, there are no right answers in such an activity; there is instead the discussion about what seems to be important and why. This activity immediately generates interest as students seek to justify their selections, consider what they know and do not yet know about American history, outline their criteria, and produce their final selections.

A sort can also be about qualities or values suggested by a question. For example, a sort which addresses the topic *What's good for kids?* could include among the 70 to 80 choices items such as:

television in their bedroom
a stay-at-home mom
music lessons
tennis lessons
no toy guns
religious school
martial arts lessons
grandparents nearby
strict discipline
weekly chores
allowance
no allowance
clothes allowance
babysitting for siblings
school with uniforms
school that is child-centered

A sort like this might be useful in a child development course, or in advisories, or in an English class focused on adolescent literature.

Panels are another way to generate discussion and interest. Including a strongly opinionated speaker (especially someone whose ideas run counter to the majority opinion) or a group of individuals who represent divergent opinions can be used to highlight differences and foster student responses. For example, a panel that might follow up the previous sort on *What's good for kids?* could include parents from various cultures and backgrounds who raise their children in different ways. Students might be invited to ask a parent to participate or staff might ask their own parents to talk about their child-rearing ideas. Again, it's the difference in approaches, from lenient to strict, that would make the panel interesting for the students and encourage them to get involved in a discussion at the conclusion.

Below is another suggestion for a panel, one that might encourage students to do more reading. The question for the panel, *Is it important to read over the summer?* could be useful at the end or the beginning of the school year. Three positions on this question might be:

POSITION 1: We are a nation of sheep—of non-readers. Because of our nation's poor reading habits we are at the mercy of advertisers and unscrupulous politicians. People who don't read, and instead watch TV or play video games all the time, don't learn to think critically. Then, we get poor government and the corruption we deserve.

POSITION 2: You overstate the importance of reading. It's not the only thing in life. If you attend school regularly and do OK on the SAT, that's enough. You can get whatever information you need from TV and the Internet.

POSITION 3: Neither position is correct. Yes, you should read books to be well informed and not depend on TV, but different kids have different learning styles. Some kids are just not interested in reading—you need balance in life so you shouldn't make judgments or form assumptions about people who don't read a lot.

VIDEO CLIPS Another way to initiate discussion is to present a series of video clips (about five minutes in length) from feature films that relate to a common theme. For example, in a project that examined the definition and purpose of community, the unit began with the screening of selected excerpts that offered divergent ways of describing community. The videos included scenes from:

Witness: the barn raising scene which shows Amish farmers helping one another.

School Daze: the town gown conflict raises questions about conflicting communities.

Breakfast Club: the students who begin as distant from one another form a tight group by the end.

Rocky: patriotism acts as a factor in binding people together.

Parting Glances: AIDS underscores a sense of community among gay people.

Students view the film clips, then discuss in small groups their definition of community and what purpose it seems to serve. Comments are then brought to the full group for further conversation.

DEBATE

Almost any interesting topic lends itself to debate, even subjects that might seem quite sophisticated. In an economics class, a teaching colleague could join the classroom teacher to debate the need for government regulation (vs. a free market) as a way to unpack basic economic concepts and engage students in discussion.

Or, an English class might begin an examination of recommended college preparatory reading lists with a debate between the classroom teacher and a colleague. One might take the position that the "great books" approach is overly dependent on books by dead white men while the opponent might argue that contemporary multicultural literature panders to the current "fashion" and is of poor quality when measured by classical standards. They might also debate whether a list of recommended books must always strike a balance between the number of men and women writers, or whether the best story should always prevail, regardless of authorship. Another debatable topic might question whether time periods matter in selecting recommended reading—should older books dominate? Should contemporary literature ever be included if we do not yet know it will stand the test of time?

Again, the idea behind the debates is to bring students into the conversation and to foster their interest and curiosity.

CONVERSATIONS

A carefully selected speaker—such as a private investigator, actor, musician, sports writer—can often provoke interesting questions and help students think about issues (even careers) in new ways. It's often a good idea to limit the speaker's presentation to ten minutes (perhaps furnishing students with a brief bio in advance) and to leave the rest of the time available for questions and discussion.

Initially, students will need to discover that they, not the teacher, are responsible for asking the questions. The teacher will want to keep track of questions and responses in order to provide students with material for a follow-up discussion. (See section on note taking, page 31.)

(See section on note taking, page 31.)

THE LIST:
KEEPING TRACK OF DISCUSSION

"We can all learn from each other—so if someone has something to say that I disagree with, by the end of the class they might have changed my entire opinion because they have stronger points or did more reading and have more evidence to support their point of view."

Melissa, student

Genuine discussion usually results in a lively debate, so the teacher will need to maintain a list of students who want to speak. To facilitate an orderly process no matter how wildly students' hands may be waving, each student receives the same response: Your name is on the list. Students learn to respect the list, as they see that it applies to all equally. And eventually, everyone does get their chance to speak.

The list obviates the need for the teacher to be constantly refereeing between forceful students who jockey for speaking time. It also reassures quieter students that they don't have to enter a fray to be acknowledged—a simple raising of the hand will do. Most importantly, it frees the students of all that extra "drama" and allows them to apply their energy to listening to each other. When they do, discussion becomes genuine, as students begin to reflect not only on what they have to say but on what they have heard.

"Ever since I began in this school I have been told to take notes, take notes, take notes—whether on a legal pad or on my hand, I write down the ideas that are expressed or what I want to say."

Marcela, student

Inquiry-based discussion requires active participation for both the students and the teacher. Note taking is an essential ingredient of this process. Inquiry teachers regularly advise students to write down points they want to make so that they won't forget them by the time they get to speak. Students will often disregard this advice, until their name comes up on the list and they've forgotten what it was they wanted to say. From then on, they become note takers. They learn to take notes not just from points the teacher makes, but comments made by other students during the discussion, a skill that will do them well once they get to college (and one that most students from information-based schools lack).

Their notes also become important references for the papers they will be writing. (See page 32 for more information about the link between discussion and writing.)

Teachers also take notes during discussions. Often, while fulfilling the role of moderator for a discussion, teachers forget what some of the most interesting comments are since they're also focused on keeping the discussion going, coming up with thought-provoking questions, jotting down the names of those who want to speak, watching the clock to check how much time is left to the period, and wanting to get in a good explanation of the homework assignment—all this while still focusing on Jesse, hoping to see a chance to bring him into the conversation, and stopping everything in order to clarify or provide some evidence that might help support a more nuanced point of view.

Who said that insightful comment about the author's intent? Which student challenged that statement? What was the quotation that Maria used? So! How can a teacher keep track of all this? It's extremely helpful to keep notes on what has been said: quick jottings of where the conversation might go, reminders of points that you want to be sure get introduced, ideas about future paper topics that might help students tie everything together, a record of what's been said and by whom.

See the Appendix for samples of teacher's notes from two different classes. They offer examples of how a teacher may use this technique while discussion ensues.

SPEAKING AS A TOOL FOR WRITING

"Over and over, you see how discussion helps kids become better writers. We do a lot of writing: some teachers have kids write in class, others assign narratives, analytic papers, research papers. That's true across the curriculum."

Herb Mack, principal

The link between speaking and writing is an important feature of any worthwhile writing program. Both are expressions of thought and each helps to clarify the other. Too many schools embark on a drive to improve students' writing and completely neglect the fact that talk and discussion inspire and nurture good writing. To ask students to compose essays and research papers deprived of the benefits of discussion is to seriously limit what they might achieve.

Discussion-based classrooms have none of that problem. Students use talk in the classroom to explore, delve into, analyze, and clarify. They do this throughout the semester; they do it before writing their papers, while reworking them, when meeting with other students in small groups or with teachers to discuss their papers and revise them.

Students' culminating papers also provide the closure that makes sense of the semester's work. Just looking at some of the topics of final papers provides insight into the larger mission of a class:

> What sort of speech can be censored under the United States Constitution?
>
> Did heroes create the Civil Rights Movement or did the Movement create the heroes?
>
> What evidence do we have that animals can think?
>
> Is comedy tragic? Is tragedy comical?
>
> How do you find the parabolic path of a comet as it moves through the solar system?
>
> Using the height of the Statue of Liberty, what is the distance from the Manhattan berth of the Staten Island ferry to the Staten Island berth?

DEVIL'S ADVOCATE POSITION Either the teacher or a student may want to play "devil's advocate," making sure to represent a view that is not being expressed by other students and that may, in fact, run counter to what the majority of the students are saying. As an intellectual activity, this technique manages to get all the students engaged. With the knowledge that they are "playing" with an idea, even one that they may be skeptical of, students allow themselves to investigate the idea and its ramifications in more depth. The distancing from an emotional stance helps open up their mindset to other possibilities. Although they may not change their basic point of view, they may nevertheless come away with a greater understanding of how someone may hold an opinion that is different from their own.

Some very basic techniques help to reinforce the goal of students talking and listening to other students:

- Place students' chairs in a circle so they can face each other when they speak.
- Note down what particular students say and quote the students during discussion.
- Redirect comments and questions to the students—let them take responsibility for responding or answering or providing evidence.
- Act as a tape recorder and "playback" some of the students' comments—help keep the thread of discussion clear so students don't lose track of the main point.
- Type up notes on discussion with kids' names and distribute the next day for comments.

DISCUSSION IN MATH CLASSES

"When they work in small groups they will catch each other's mistakes— if a student takes a step that doesn't make sense, that's illogical, they watch and discuss what is happening. For students who do know the material, they will be solidifying their own understanding of the problem by talking about it. That also works for the student who needs to ask more questions, try things out, and bounce ideas off other students."

Becky Walzer, teacher

Although teachers may readily see the possibilities, indeed the benefits, for discussion in literature, history, and science classrooms, they may find it hard to imagine using discussion in teaching math. Typically, math classes follow a predictable format with the teacher demonstrating problems at the board and the students doing similar problems on their own and for homework. There is little discussion, save for some questions most likely asked by students who already are partially knowledgeable about the problems being presented. But those who are lost remain lost unless they are fortunate enough to have tutors.

A discussion-based classroom in math addresses the weaknesses of the typical math class. An important feature is the use of small groups. With students working in groups of three, there are opportunities for students to share ideas about how to solve a problem, catch errors that others in their group may miss, and challenge and support each other. Of course, the composition of groups becomes a delicate job for the teacher. Ideally, the students in a group are of equal skill so that no one dominates the conversation. Also, the teacher has to balance the temperaments of the students in the group. Once groups are structured, teachers can make changes and adjustments as students progress.

Another feature distinguishes the discussion-based math classroom: problems may be presented for solving before the students have been instructed in a method for solving them. Thus, students need to discuss possible solutions and try out ideas, using logic and the math skills they have to test their proposals. What they learn through these exercises is the possibility of solving problems through a number of approaches and formulations, which they will be called upon to explain to other students. In this way, math class too becomes a discussion-based classroom.

As with all experiences in discussion, the more students participate in such math classes, the more access they have to other students already familiar and comfortable with the expectations of discussion-based classes, the more they exhibit the behaviors and attitudes that help such classrooms succeed.

6

How Can Students Be Prepared for Discussion?

"To speak, there's a list and you have to get on that list . . . I heard those rules, I saw them in every class—that's where I learned the discussion rules."

Marjorie, student

The best way to prepare students for discussion-based classes is to create opportunities for other students to train them. That is facilitated by having ungraded classrooms.

Every freshman who participates in a classroom with sophomores, juniors, and seniors learns immediately what the responsibilities of the student are in a discussion-based classroom. The new student observes first-hand that other students are actively involved, that there are rules (like "the list," respect for differences of opinion, "no personal attacks"), that there are expectations ("what is your evidence?"), and that older students—those whom a younger student would naturally look up to for clues as to how to behave in this new environment—take their responsibility as discussion participants seriously.

For those schools that cannot use an ungraded format, modifications are possible. For example, 9th and 10th graders can be combined, thus automatically ensuring that every class will have seasoned discussion participants to provide role models. Schools using this model have also found it beneficial to combine 11th and 12th graders in classes. Another option is to designate a select group of classes as ungraded, as happens frequently at the college level. Schools have found it extremely helpful to have ungraded math classes, for example.

Most importantly, even if no arrangement for an ungraded classroom is possible, discussion can still thrive in a classroom. It will probably take students longer to trust that their voices are valued, but with time and practice, and some of the techniques we've mentioned here to structure the process and encourage quieter students, classrooms can become discussion-based. As students become more adept and comfortable with the format, they and their teacher will notice a shift in the culture of the classroom and students' readiness to participate.

7　How Can Teachers Be Prepared to Lead Discussion?

"The teacher who says he has covered the material usually means he has talked about the material, and he's had students read about it. But he often has no idea of which kid was simply looking out the window thinking about his birthday. However, if inquiry is working, I am hearing what the kids are thinking . . . I'm hearing them thinking."

Herb Mack, principal

The best way for new teachers to learn more about discussion-based classes is to observe one. New teachers should be provided with time in their schedules to sit in on experienced teachers' classes, to meet with them, to discuss with other teachers the difficulties of coming up with good questions, to share questions and techniques that have worked well as "openers," and to observe practiced teachers' techniques for sustaining discussion.

The greater the number of teachers in a school who adhere to the discussion-based model, the more students learn to accept its protocol and relish the opportunities it offers them. And the more adept students are at participating in such classes, the quicker a new teacher learns how to balance the complex demands of a discussion-based classroom.

This film and booklet should also help introduce teachers to the ideas and practices of discussion-based classrooms.

What Are the Particular Difficulties of Teaching a Discussion-Based Class?

TOLERATING AMBIGUITIES

Teachers need to learn the most difficult lesson of all: allowing time for a discussion to unfold. A teacher's instinct is to rush in to cover the endless amount of material that exists or to correct a perceived wrong in a student's response. But in an inquiry classroom, lessons will not be as straightforward as in an information-based classroom. Discussions may meander or break off before a clear resolution is reached. This is not unusual, and it may take some time for a teacher to become comfortable with the ambiguities inherent in an approach where discussion is central to a lesson.

NOT KNOWING ALL THE ANSWERS

If teachers must know all there is to know about the many topics they feel obligated to cover, they will, by necessity, need to limit discussion and questions lest they wind up in unfamiliar and unchartered terrain.

However, if both the teacher and the students accept that the teacher cannot possibly have all the answers, then students must assume some of the responsibility for stretching their thinking beyond the superficial and acquiring greater knowledge. They must probe, and explore, and think; they must gather evidence and weigh it and come to conclusions.

"It can be hard to listen to the silence but I have to give them time to put their ideas together. I have to remember that I'm asking them sophisticated questions. It might take a couple of minutes to synthesize what's going on and to think about how they want to respond."

Cathy Tomaszewski

Difficult and challenging questions ought to require some quiet time for thinking. Teachers need to learn to trust the silence. Time must be allotted for discussion to unfold.

Silent students also must be afforded time to become familiar with a discussion-based classroom. It's not unusual for some students to take their time—maybe even two years—before they'll take the plunge and participate in discussion. This is not their failing nor the teacher's. And their silence doesn't mean withdrawal from the thinking that's going on. The quiet student needs to be respected for that right. It's not unusual to see the quietest students writing the most thoughtful papers and those who are only too eager to speak having the greatest challenge when it's time to write. Each student has strengths and weaknesses.

Although observers of classrooms are often counseled to keep track of how many students have spoken and to critique teachers who have not managed to get every student to participate in a particular class discussion, they are missing the point. There are lots of reasons kids don't talk in class. The goal is not quantity but quality, and not just who is speaking, but who is listening. Teachers will often complain that it's not that they can't get kids to talk, it's that they can't get them to listen to each other.

Experienced teachers have developed a number of practices to help students take the plunge and speak in class. One technique may be to circulate a sheet of paper and ask each student to write down one or two thoughts they have on a given topic and then read some of those ideas, anonymously, aloud in class. In time, the shy student may announce ownership of the idea and then go on to explain it. Or that student may just whisper to the teacher, getting ready to speak aloud one day to the class. One teacher suggests taking students aside at another time during the day and saying casually, "I can tell you're doing the reading and have lots of ideas I can tell by your tests and homeworks. We'd really like to hear your ideas in class, too." Sometimes it's the most casual asides that are the most encouraging to students. Teachers experienced with discussion-based teaching know the value of acknowledging a good homework or a comment offered in class, whether said aloud or written in a student's midterm or final report.

RELINQUISHING CLOSURE

Too often the need for closure cuts off deeper exploration of a topic. In a discussion-based classroom, synthesizing and summarizing are ongoing activities, but not necessarily at the conclusion of each class period. By the end of the semester, however, students are ready for closure and in their conversations and papers, will be creating their own as well.

ADJUSTING FOR CLASS SIZE

All teachers would prefer small classes—maybe 15 or 18 students. But not all are so fortunate. Class size, however, should not limit the practice of discussion-based lessons. Although seating students in a circle is the best arrangement for discussion since students can easily look at each other when they respond to what each other has said, comparable seating arrangements are possible for larger groups. If needed, two concentric circles could be set up. This seating arrangement immediately signals to students that talking and listening to each other is valued and practiced in this particular classroom.

Large classes have the advantage of producing more points of view and differences of opinion about issues, reading materials, ideas, and problem-solving. And it's the exchange of ideas that is central to a successful discussion-based classroom, whether in literature, science, history, math, or art classes.

COUNTERACTING THE PRESSURES OF HIGH STAKES TESTS

The life of the classroom and the judgment of teachers are not immune to the pressures of the current high stakes testing environment. Responsible teachers, even though they understand the flaws and dangers of high stakes exams, still feel compelled to help their students pass. The mistake is to equate passing these exams with anything approaching meaningful learning. Test prep is not teaching. Mastering test taking skills is not inquiry learning. If teachers decide their students need help with standardized tests, they need to make explicit distinctions between teaching and learning and test preparation.

We would suggest confining test prep to a specific amount of time—perhaps for three weeks or a month—while preserving the majority of the semester for developing a discussion-based curriculum. Despite the pressures placed on students and teachers by state and local administrators, teachers should not sacrifice what they know to be meaningful learning and engaging curriculum for an onslaught of test prep.

If teachers decide that their students will need more than an end-of-term concentrated test prep period, they still need to make explicit the distinction between test prep lessons and real study and learning. Making the distinction is, in itself, a means to teach students about the value and pleasure of education versus the standardization of state-mandated exams.

A P P E N D I X

Sample teacher's notes from social studies class

Discussion topic: Two different authors' perspectives on the Civil War

*"The notes I'm taking are students' responses to the questions I've asked. . . .
If someone says something either to disagree or elaborate, I can go back to
the notes and tie things together."*

Avram Barlowe, teacher

*   *   *

*Damon: text Line/Doug debate p. 4 skillful spkr. complex-simple
big part contradicts p.10 2 speech N/S Ill.*

*Shaniqua: generally more fallible, not great man who ends
slavery reality stuck in the middle please this/that side*

Monique: agr not like most texts, more of a pol.

*Elana: AL just might have been doing it for polit reasons, 2
get elected and then do something*

Damon: white men seeing blks inferior. Yes, brilliant but no passion for fighting for Blacks

Milav: politics form of biz. AL what slaves could do for him-vote

Drew: Don't see how he talks out of both sides of mouth. Said he was against spread of slavery to new states, not abol/equal

Molly: (Drew) last page unite as one people, equal. Next column no-clear contradiction

Shaniqua: that's how pol work, what they do he did have a passion but if wanted to be elected can't be abolitionist. Evid: 1849 D.C. abol/fugit. Slaves-both sides

Molly: diff btwn. riding the fence and what AL did-saying opposite things

Damon: talk both sides means no passion

Shaniqua: talk both sides have passion get elected

ME-Linc's comments racist?

Rafiq: AL more strategic, blk abols too viol evid: text

Molly: Linc-politics w/in syst. JB violence; politics not working-war

Rafiq: evidence p.8 abs limited. Lincoln in better posit

Teresa: not racist, objective how it was

Monique: racist time

Molly: who knows? need letters, journals

Elana: not racist back then racist not a word slavery?

Damon: racism is racism regardless of time; slavery is wrong/racist whenever no justif. W/B not equal racist and wrong

Manuel: Maybe AL wanted to free slaves and not scare whites so sounded racist. Whites think freedom-black takeover

ME: Why North? Pp. 6/10

Teresa: (Damon) not justifying slavery. AL words work today

Shaniqua: times change, can be not racist in yr time standards change, women's dresses hemlines, ankle, knee

Milav: free, but no justice, no ed., pick cotton

1. Shaniqua v. Damon - AL slick, smart pol. v. AL wishy-washy

2. Rafiq v. Manuel - free, unequal, anti-slavery but racist v. free but don't scare whites

3. Milav/Damon v. Shaniqua/Monique is freedom w/out equality better than slavery?

Damon: If no slavery, then no racism. Word not exist? Where did work come from? Slavery. What power do you have if you can't vote, can't walk street freely, still oppressed even worse in some ways

Shaniqua: disagree freedom no master I own you. Parents house guardians make rules. Out of house-no job, hard but at least don't tell you what to do.

Damon: no comparison. I'm not a slave in my parents house!

Nancy: hope, potential, possibility

Damon: slave had it too

Rafiq: back 2 faces of Lincoln, can be anti-slavery and racist

ME: Northern opposition-moral or economic reasons?

Sample teacher's notes from English class
Discussion topic: opening discussion about "ghetto literature"

"The notes act both as a record of the discussion and a tool to be used to keep the discussion going."

Gail Lemelbaum, teacher

*   *   *

What is a "ghetto story"?

James: characters—no motivation

Julie: misused talent

Kenny: getting out!

basketball one way out

Marcela: hope—another symbol

Julie: minorities without hope

Angela: earn $ by any means

James: not much to lose

    desperation

Tanisha: watch TV, want stuff & $

Muhammad: do what you have to do to survive

Kenny: Notice characters [in "ghetto story novels"]: drug dealer, prostitutes

    James: learning survival skills

      bad schools

      get bad advice

    Angela: but level-headed mother

Questions raised by kids during discussion—could be writing topic:

    Is James [character in novel] a good dad?

    Why is pride more important than food?

    Should they have gone on relief?

Possible topic: Relationship between poverty and alcoholism

Kids focus on Money—everything revolves around $

    Tanisha: goal to be middle class

Jordan: ego/emotional survival

supporting the family

Job=Pride

men in books respond differently than women

Need to show they're a man

Question kids discuss heatedly: <u>What characterizes a good father?</u>

PICK UP THIS THEME WITH NEXT BOOK

Get back to money theme with next book

Next class:

Girls discussing Sexual abuse & poverty—Sukie [character in novel]

Princess: Inequality

Girls think this the way to get $

James (another perspective): Glad you don't live in novel's neighborhood

They don't deserve their fate

Questions: Whose life is harder: males or females?

Writing on gender and character and effects of ghetto

Whites fear blacks—newspaper stories in the novel

 Who reads the newspapers?

 Conformity

 not relevant to people in the hood

Muhammad: life in Projects—unhealthy places

 things haven't changed much

Princess: story shows disciplining by hitting

Jamil—characters feel overwhelmed, trapped

 Lose hope

 end of novel-hopelessness, no change

Tanisha—worse, realizing no change will happen

 on going cycle

Angela—But there is growth in Francie [character] even in her
 neighborhood

 physical changes, becoming a woman

 ealizes she's unhappy

 the _realizing_ is important

 lost respect for her dad

Princess—not afraid of Sukie

Questions to follow up: Value of dreams, hope when environment has collapsed around you-when family supports are gone . . .

Kenny—anger is a way to survive, not dreams

Next class

Value of gangs when you grow up in the ghetto

James—Sterling was promising student, but no future

Kenny—need protection, be accepted-anger brings together

sense of family

Angela—but mother pleads

Marcela—period of the novel, no exposure to others

closed environment